PROJECT GOSHEN
and the
Garden of Eden

UNDER A NEW
COVENANT LENS

Naomi Carmelo Hernandez

ISBN 979-8-89309-136-6 (Paperback)
ISBN 979-8-89309-137-3 (Digital)

Copyright © 2024 Naomi Carmelo Hernandez
All rights reserved
First Edition

All rights reserved. No part of this publication may be reproduced, distributed, or transmitted in any form or by any means, including photocopying, recording, or other electronic or mechanical methods without the prior written permission of the publisher. For permission requests, solicit the publisher via the address below.

Covenant Books
11661 Hwy 707
Murrells Inlet, SC 29576
www.covenantbooks.com

Dedication

In loving memory and heartfelt tribute to the saints who have journeyed onward to be with our mighty Jesus, my grandparents—Paul Dawson and Mary Lou Francis Dominy and W. R. and Bobbie Jean Roper. Your legacy of faith, prayers, and inspiration continues to inspire and guide us.

To my beloved parents, Paul Wayne and Mary Jean Dominy, whose unwavering support and invaluable contributions have helped shape the distinct purpose of this book. I am forever grateful. Your guidance and love have equipped me to share the treasures within these pages with the world.

To my husband, Mateo Carmelo Hernandez, who, through it all, was very supportive.

To my aunts and uncles, who have contributed through this life's journey, as well as my siblings and children.

I extend my heartfelt gratitude to Apostle Todd Smith and Dr. Karen Smith for their profound spiritual gifts and guided teachings, serving as nurturing figures and spiritual parents in the house of God at Christ Fellowship Church in Dawsonville, Georgia. And how could I forget Pastor Sherrie Potts for her encouraging sisterhood. She signifies a relationship characterized by empathy and mutual respect marked by wonderful support—her shared laughter, a shoulder to lean on in times of need, and so much more.

Above all, I dedicate this work to the Holy Spirit, whose divine presence illuminates every word and infuses it with purpose and power.

Contents

Foreword ix
Preface xiii
Chapter 1: Reflecting from Impermanence to Transcending Logical Thinking 1
Chapter 2: Walking in Wisdom and Faith 12
Chapter 3: Inheritance of Wisdom 32
Chapter 4: Stewarding Someone Else's Property 42
Chapter 5: Being Wise 57
Chapter 6: God Preparing Me in a Warning 79
Chapter 7: A Glimpse of Gardening Techniques 102
Organic Gardening for Beginners 107

Foreword

I met Mrs. Hernandez and her family at Christ Fellowship Church, Dawsonville, where we worship and have served together for several years. When there is a need that involves attending to others, their response is always "Yes, we will be there." As a family, they are committed to fulfilling a call to minister well and without hesitation.

Christ Fellowship is home to the North Georgia Revival, a unique immersion ministry work birthed and sustained by prayer and the precious presence of our Father. We have spent many Sunday evenings and into the early morning hours tending to hundreds of dear souls. Naomi serves consistently and with compassion from beginning to end, month after month, year after year. It is a commitment she genuinely embraces and just one example of her service-oriented lifestyle.

Naomi is a lifelong student of the scriptures. She is a searcher and is driven by a persistent, authentic desire to be equipped for any opportunity to minister to the Lord. In conversations with her, it is immediately apparent that her heart posture is humble, yet resolute. She is eager to exhort and encourage others. She is careful to seek wisdom from the Holy Spirit as to accomplishing that mandate. And she listens.

Whenever Naomi comes to mind, I think of a seasoned believer with a deliberate objective to motivate others to honor God and make the most of every moment of *this life.* And I think of a daughter of God who has counted the cost and embraced the responsibility of presenting this book to Him and to you.

I invite you to glean from Naomi's inspired perspective!

Sherrie Potts, staff pastor / executive business administrator / immersion ministry team leader / prayer ministry team leader, Christ Fellowship Church Dawsonville, Georgia

Preface

Amid the chaos and uncertainty of our world, there exists a beacon of hope—a timeless truth that has the power to transform lives and bring solace to troubled hearts. This book is born out of a deep conviction that in God's Word lies the key to not only surviving but thriving amid adversity.

The inspiration behind this work stems from a profound desire to reach out to a generation, perhaps even to those who have long traversed this earth yet remain unaware of the transformative power of God's promises. In the pages that follow, we embark on a journey to explore the riches of God's new covenant and the profound impact it can have on our lives.

At its core, this book is a call to action—a call to embrace the truth that God's Word is living and active, and when applied with faith, it yields abundant fruit. Through the lens of scripture, we will discover the unwavering assurance that God's promises never return void. They are not mere words on a page but living truths that have the power to sustain us in the darkest of times.

As we navigate the clamorous waters of this fallen world, let us take heart in the promise that God is with us, leading us, and equipping us to stand firm in the face of adversity. May this book serve as a road map to understanding and applying God's Word in our daily lives, ensuring that we are firmly rooted in His truth when the storms of life rage around us. Together, let us hop on this journey of faith, knowing that as we anchor ourselves in God's promises, we find the strength, courage, and hope to overcome every obstacle that stands in our way.

With sincere gratitude and anticipation,
Naomi Carmelo Hernandez.

Reflecting from Impermanence to Transcending Logical Thinking

While on my walk, I found myself in deep contemplation about the impermanent nature of the world. I was seeking to understand the concept of the world being temporal and realized the importance of shifting away from logical thinking. The Lord had previously impressed upon me the significance of rising above logical thinking.

In light of the world's temporal nature, it's essential to remember that originally, the world was created for humanity to have dominion over it. However, when humanity fell, a curse was brought upon us.

Reference: Genesis 3:14–19 (MSG)

GOD told the serpent: "Because you've done this, you're cursed, cursed beyond all cattle and wild animals, Cursed to slink on your belly and eat dirt all your life. I'm declaring war between you and the Woman, between your offspring and hers. He'll wound your head, you'll wound his heel."

He told the Woman: "I'll multiply your pains in childbirth; you'll give birth to your babies in pain. You'll want to please your husband, but he'll lord it over you."

He told the Man: "Because you listened to your wife and ate from the tree That I commanded you not to eat from, 'Don't eat from this tree,' The very ground is cursed because of you; getting food from the ground Will be as painful as having babies is for your wife; you'll be working in pain all your life long. The ground will sprout thorns and weeds, you'll get your food the hard way, Planting and tilling and harvesting, sweating in the fields from dawn to dusk, Until you return to that ground yourself, dead and buried; you started out as dirt, you'll end up dirt."

This leads me to the following:

> Christ has redeemed us from the curse of the law, having become a curse for us (for it is written, "Cursed is everyone who hangs on a tree"), that the blessing of Abraham might come upon the Gentiles in Christ Jesus, that we might receive

> the promise of the Spirit
> through faith. (Galatians
> 3:13–14 NKJV)

This means, first, Jesus did this by taking on those consequences himself when he was crucified. And second of all, this act allows non-Jews, which are the Gentiles, to receive the same blessings that were promised to Abraham. And through faith in Jesus, everyone can receive the Holy Spirit, which is a special gift from God. Overall, the passage emphasizes that through Jesus everyone can be saved and receive God's blessings, not those who follow just the Jewish law.

> Stand fast therefore in
> the liberty by which Christ

has made us free, and do not be entangled again with a yoke of bondage. (Galatians 5:1 NKJV)

Jesus has set us free from the strict rules and regulations of the old religious laws.

Go to the time when the Father sent His Son, Jesus, as the promised seed. Jesus came in the flesh to redeem us from sin, fulfilling the Old Testament foreshadowing of sacrifice, including the blood offerings in the Tabernacle. He, as the High Priest, represented the Royal Priest and became the Living Sacrifice, the Lamb Whose blood was sprinkled on the mercy seat to redeem and forgive us of all our sins. In doing so, He shattered the curse that weighed upon humanity.

Unfortunately, many of us have failed to recognize that this curse has been broken and lifted. This happens because we sometimes choose to return to the old ways. Not knowing this looks as if His sacrifice was in vain; rather, it reflects our lack of understanding and knowledge.

God sums this up in Hosea.

Reference: Hosea 4:6

> My people are destroyed from lack of knowledge. Because you have rejected knowledge, I also reject you as my priests; because you have ignored the law of your

God, I also will ignore your children.

This verse is highlighting the importance of knowing and following God's teachings, and the serious consequences of neglecting them.

Through His sacrifice, Jesus broke the curse on the cross. It's important to note that when people speak of curses, it's often a result of their own choices or ignorance to pick them up. We were set free by Christ's sacrifice, and it is His desire for us to walk in the freedom He has redeemed us for, aligning with His original divine plan. At its core, this is a call to action—a call to embrace the truth that God's Word is living and active, and when applied with faith, it yields abundant fruit. They are not mere words on a page but living truths that have the power to sustain us in the darkest of times. First and foremost, you must be born again.

With God's tremendous agape love, His Son suffered and died for us. I want Him to receive the full reward of His suffering. In doing so, we must rightly divide the word of God, apply it, and teach others what it really meant for Him to redeem us and to grant us blessings while we are still on earth. Allow me to emphasize this once again. My dad said it best. Signs and wonders are to follow the believer, not the believer to follow signs and wonders. *Believers* refer to "you are of God, little children, and have overcome them because He who is in you is greater than he who is in the world."

Unbelievers refer to "they are of the world; therefore, they speak as of the world, and the world hears them" (1 John 4:5 NKJV). See James 1:8 of the Bible, which describes a double-minded person is "unstable in all his ways." This verse completes an idea that James introduced in verse 5, which says that God promises wisdom to those who ask for it, but we must believe and not doubt. The verse also says that we should not seek wisdom from sources contrary to God, and we should not weigh God's wisdom against others (BibleRef.com).

The Bible defines a double-minded man in James 1:7–8 as someone who doubts and compares them to a wave of the sea that is blown and tossed by the wind. The verse says that such a person should not expect to receive anything from the Lord (Bible Study Tools). Thanks for the teaching on this, Dad. This opened my eyes for certain.

Where we are today is our own fault. We should have been properly taught to pray. The Bible commands us to pray for one another and live by the word under the right division of it.

Walking in Wisdom and Faith

Confess your trespasses to one another, and pray for one another, that you may be healed. The effective, fervent prayer of a righteous man avails much.

—James 5:16 NKJV

Our laziness in prayer, unwillingness to learn, and failure to stand up for the truth is the result of what we are facing in these last days.

My dad hosted a Bible study on a Tuesday night at his home. It happened a week after I received a word from the Lord urging me to stop relying on logical thinking and instead have faith in Him. The message was clear: shift from worldly thinking to a mindset centered solely on the Lord. Interestingly, my dad's teachings echoed this theme, emphasizing the idea of entering the realm of Jesus. He highlighted how Jesus dwells in us, and we in Him, which should lead to a departure from logical thinking and a deeper embrace of faith in the Lord.

He *referenced 2 Peter 1:2–4 (NLT)*:

> May God give you more and more grace and peace as you grow in your knowledge of God and Jesus our Lord. By his divine power God has given us everything we need for living a godly life.

We have received all of this by coming to know him, the one who called us to himself by means of his marvelous glory and excellence. And because of his glory and excellence, he has given us great and precious promises. These are the promises that enable you to share his divine nature and escape the world's corruption caused by human desires.

We're reminded of the abundant grace and peace available to believers through knowing God and Jesus. This passage also highlights the concept of divine power, emphasizing God's ability to meet all our needs and empower us to live godly lives. Additionally, it speaks of the precious promises given to believers, such as eternal life and the indwelling of the Holy Spirit, which provide hope and assurance in our journey of faith and discuss our participation in the divine nature. Dad emphasized that "if we are in the divine nature of his power, then why are we walking around busted and disgusted and sick and broke?" He questioned, "Why, if we possess this divine nature?" And he's right. We often struggle with sickness, poverty, and other issues. He challenged us to break free from limiting beliefs and recognize the immense power within us, waiting to be unleashed.

Refer to 2 Peter 1:2–4 again, because I would like to emphasize something. These verses highlight the multiplication of grace and peace through knowledge of God and Jesus, and how God's divine power has provided everything needed for life and godliness. It speaks of the great promises given to believers, enabling them to partake in the divine nature and escape the corruption of the world.

Reference: 2 Corinthians 7:1 (NLT)

> Because we have these promises, dear friends, let us cleanse ourselves from everything that can defile our body or spirit. And let us work toward complete holiness because we fear God.

God's love for us is immeasurable. He didn't send His Son to suffer and die for us because we were worthless. Quite the contrary, He did it because of His profound love for us. Our current predicament isn't due to His lack of love; it's our own doing. Our negligence in prayer, laziness to learn, and failure to stand up for the truth—these have contributed to the challenges we face as a result.

All this ties back to the scripture that reminds us of the thief who steals, kills, and destroys.

Reference: John 10:10

> The thief comes only to steal and kill and destroy. I have come that they may

have life and have it to the full.

He has been robbing us of our true identity from the very beginning—just like how he attempted to challenge Jesus's identity in the desert, and Jesus responded, "It is written."

Reference: Matthew 4:10–11

> Then saith Jesus unto him, Get thee hence, Satan: for it is written, Thou shalt worship the Lord thy God, and him only shalt thou serve. Then the devil leaveth him, and, behold, angels

came and ministered unto him.

The devil is a liar! See John 8:44 (NLT)—it talks about where he was a murderer from the beginning. He always hated the truth because there is no truth in him. When he lies, it is consistent. He is a liar and the father of lies.

While much of this conversation revolves around the idea of temptation in Matthew that I just referenced, it's essential to recognize that the enemy's primary goal is to steal our identity. This emphasizes the importance of understanding our true identity in Christ, knowing our worth, and recognizing the blessings we have because of Him. By embracing our identity in Him, we can stand firm against the enemy's deceitful lies and walk confidently in His truth, and in what He has for us.

Understanding the blessings that the Lord paid for on the cross and the fact that we can walk in what He has for us is the reason I'm writing this book and want to start this project. I feel a calling to reach out to those who have been neglected for such a time as this, to impart knowledge about living a more abundant life while we journey through this earthly realm. We can thrive with the blessings that God has given us—blessings that are well within our reach. Unfortunately, our worldly mindset has been desensitized to believe we need government permission for everything. I'm not suggesting undermining authority, but I want to emphasize that

Project Goshen and the Garden of Eden

such thinking is rooted in brainwashing. It's crucial to understand that when humanity fell, we were meant to reclaim what was lost because Christ broke the curse upon the tree. His words "speak life" signify the restoration of God's abundant blessings. Recall what happened when man fell and the devil deceived. Refer to *Genesis 3:13–15 NLT*.

So we must stand up to reclaim the dominion that was originally meant for us, God's children. Once you gain wisdom and seek the Father and the Holy Spirit, you'll grasp the true meaning of dominion. You'll come to understand that the entire world can be your Goshen, an Old Testament narrative under a New Testament lens—a safe haven, so to speak. So we often study the lack of wisdom, as in *Hosea 4:6* where it's mentioned that "my people die due to a lack of knowledge."

Understanding Key Biblical Moments: Sin, Consequence, and Redemption

I brought Genesis 3:15 up again to show you this. He's talking about God saying there will be ongoing hostility between the serpent and the woman representing evil to the woman. The hostility will extend to their descendants. Of course, they've been redeemed by the Lord under the new covenant, when they accept him for their salvation called born again.

Watch Your Mouth

Refer also to *Proverbs 30:32 NLT*.

> If you have been a fool by being proud or plotting evil, cover your mouth in shame.

This proverb is telling us that if you have acted foolishly by being arrogant or planning to do something bad, you should recognize it. You should be ashamed of yourself and stop talking. It is advising people to recognize their mistakes especially when they involve pride or evil intentions and to feel remorse for their actions.

Also check out *Proverbs 18:21 NKJV*.

> Death and life *are* in the power of the tongue, and those who love it will eat its fruit.

You should not allow your words to cut you off from God's blessings. Avoid confessing negative thoughts; instead, speak life into every situation around you. The garden of Eden is a significant biblical concept down in the book of Genesis.

The Great I Am has the power to create a world and form a man out of dust, breathing life into him. Refer to Genesis 1:1–2 and Genesis 1:27, the making of man. Once you gain wisdom and seek the Father and the

Holy Spirit, you'll grasp the true meaning of dominion. We often lack wisdom.

Sometimes limited faith hinders us. However, there must be a hunger to pursue these virtues. When individuals earnestly pray for wisdom and strive to deepen their faith, is when I believe that the saints play a crucial role. They answer these prayers through the guidance of the Holy Spirit, serving as protectors and mentors to those who seek deeper understanding and faith. To truly gain understanding and decipher the true meaning behind the words and promises of the Lord, we need to unravel the mysteries of the Bible. This isn't just about wanting to or loving to. Although that's important, it's also about comprehending the historical and cultural context to understand its true meaning.

As you dive into these contexts, you'll discover that Christ's work on the cross redeemed us and broke the curse, allowing us to step into His original plan by exercising dominion over the world. Again refer to *Genesis 3:13–15*, and now add *Titus 2:14–15*. Building upon the concept of redemption and dominion, another significant aspect of our faith is highlighted in Titus 2:14–15.

> He gave his life to free us from every kind of sin, to cleanse us, and to make us his very own people, totally committed to doing good deeds. You must teach these things and encourage the believers to do them. You

have the authority to correct them when necessary, so don't let anyone discard what you say or look down on you for doing this.

He meant it when He said we have dominion over this world. This brings me to what I believe and want to share with you: that God has placed me on this mission and inspired me to write this book and initiate this project to teach those who are not yet in the faith or haven't reached the levels of faith I've experienced, on how to survive according to God's biblical principles, thriving in this world. Despite the challenges and tribulations I faced during my upbringing, I'm thankful for the lessons they imparted, as we all encounter challenges in our own unique ways. This is not undermining God's supernatural provisions, but this is education while passing through this journey, especially for ones with lower levels of faith, to whom I would like to share and pass on my learnings.

Some experiences. I recently observed a group of men manually building a beautiful fence during my walk. It reminded me of the days when my dad was constructing a chicken coop. Most people in this generation wouldn't even know what a come-along is. It's a piece of equipment used to stretch wire, which we couldn't afford then, so Dad showed us manually how to stretch the wire, then he hammered in the staples to the poles instead of using a nail or staple gun. This is just one of the many things he instilled in his daughters to toughen them up. I'm grateful for his teachings, as they've prepared me for whatever challenges lie ahead. I've experienced the value of hard work firsthand, and I understand what it means to not be lazy. It's a principle I deeply appreciate that is rooted in the book of *Proverbs (13:4 NLT): "Lazy people want much but get little, but those who work hard will prosper."* Unfortunately, the government has taken away many aspects of discipline—emphasis added—which is another way they make people reliant on them. Their actions seem to go against many biblical teachings, such as God's detestation of laziness.

The fear of the Lord is indeed the beginning of wisdom, and when we replace it with fear of man, we erode the foundation of wisdom. God has chosen certain saints who possess knowledge, wisdom, and a hunger for understanding. They seek approval through diligent self-study of His Word, enabling them to live it out, teach it to others, and share it with those who lack faith. We've been equipped for this purpose. That's my goal: to share what I know. Since we've been there, it's our duty to pass on, much like the way Moses, Joshua, and Caleb did, the wisdom of sacrifice, resilience, and the profound meaning of serving Christ and living in holiness before Him. This, in turn, honors Him, for He is the Bread of Life. As the Scripture tells us, "Man cannot live on bread alone." Refer to Matthew 4:4 (NKJV).

In these end times, it's crucial to sustain ourselves with the Word of God, His truth, and His promises. So viewing the Old Testament's Goshen narrative through the lens of the New Covenant brings me to share how I acquired the experiences that have edified me to teach what I've learned about survival and get through hard times.

Inheritance of Wisdom

Back when I was a child, our family was going through a few transitions in our lives. During those days, I closely observed the practices of my grandmother on my dad's side. Mamaw, who was of Cherokee Indian descent and filled with the Holy Ghost, used to take care of us after school on occasion.

I recall a vivid memory from my childhood. My grandmother (Mamaw) lived on a street off of Clairmont Road, in Chamblee, Georgia, which was bustling with activity during my lifetime. She lived in proximity to a school called Skyland School in Atlanta. It was quite an extraordinary school, as it covered education from kindergarten through twelfth grade. I remember it was easily accessible from the street she lived on, making it a convenient location.

On the way to her house, there was a parking lot across from the house with a Hess gas station. I'm not entirely sure if it still exists today, but what I remember vividly is a flower shop within that parking lot. Every day, the flower shop would discard flowers that were on the verge of wilting, just appearing limp and withered. But that didn't discourage my grandmother. I can't help but have a heartfelt moment thinking about her. She would bend over and look into the sliding door of the dumpster where these almost-dead flowers were being tossed away. It was like a hidden treasure trove for her. My grandmother had an incredible ability to breathe life into even the most delicate and seemingly lifeless things. She had the spirit of God within her so profoundly that she could revive these discarded flowers.

I believe that's where I inherited my deep love for nurturing life from. Watching her transform those almost-dead flowers into her very own Callaway Garden. Papaw had a big garden in the backyard off old Bragg Street. And among the treasures back there as well was a plum tree that my father planted as a little boy.

Papaw and Mamaw lived life through their agricultural wisdom, a practice ingrained in them throughout their entire lives. Their way of life was remarkable. Everything in Mamaw's freezer came from the garden instead of canned goods. The food was not just delicious; it was fresh, pesticide-free, and organic. They had a deep understanding of what it meant to live off the land, guided by their unwavering faith.

Papaw was of Irish and German descent and was a devout, Spirit-filled Baptist preacher. They not only sowed seeds in the soil but also instilled spiritual seeds within their family. As a child, I observed their lives during a period of transitions. Even my grandmother on my mother's side, whom we called Granny (although some would refer to her as Granny Jean), had her own green thumb. She nurtured plants, and I enjoyed seeing her propagate and even graft them, and listened to her share her knowledge about their healing properties. For instance, one time, I learned that aloe vera would heal burns. She had a fix-all with her plants. It was a passion I deeply enjoyed, of natural healing that is.

Seeing these practices in action, witnessing the transformation of plants, and learning about their medicinal properties was a world I was drawn to and deeply appreciated. After witnessing their remarkable way of life, I began to comprehend the profound connection between faith and stewardship. Their example taught me invaluable lessons about resilience, resourcefulness, and reliance on God's provision. These foundational principles continue to guide me as I navigate life's challenges and uncertainties. Incidentally, I tried to revisit the place years later, but the properties had both been sold for airport, state, or government purposes. It was overgrown, and there was a fence that prevented me from crossing. On a side note, I once had my husband drive me there one day because I remembered a preacher's message about going back to your first love.

Reflections on Spiritual Growth

To me, that first love was my encounter with Christ when I was eight years old. It happened at the bottom step of my Holy Ghost–filled grandmother's side porch. I distinctly remember her leading me to the Lord at that young age. Many people can't say they repeated a prayer at such a tender age and meant it, but it was a transformative experience, despite not being perfect. I knew on that day I would never be the same, and that I had a lot to learn and grow in my faith journey.

I knew that there was still much growth and sanctification ahead of me, but as I looked up at the clouds that day, I found myself searching, saying, "Lord, I did it! I did it!" as if I were looking for Him. I understood that my life was forever changed in a unique way from the moment I first encountered Him at the age of eight. Most children at that age do not, but I was blessed enough to be surrounded and nurtured by a blessed foundation and fewer distractions. From then on, I always watched as her Bible lay open on her kitchen counter daily as she went back and forth to read it, which allowed me to want that and see that and make it normal for my life. One day, she turned to me and said, "Memorize as much of the Bible as you can. For one day they'll take it away, but they can never take it out of your heart and memory." I never forgot that as it really impacted me.

Fast-forward a bit. I was called to be baptized at nine years old, and I can still hear Mamaw's voice singing, "Shall we gather at the river?" That's a beautiful memory. As for my dad, I believe he was due to be deployed to Korea shortly after. He had already left for his flight that very day, but he managed to come up the hill and walk down beside a big old tree, at least that's how I remember it. I looked up as I stood in line, not yet immersed, and it felt so precious—like my earthly father joining my heavenly Father in this moment. I'm not sure what happened with his flight, whether it was canceled or delayed, but he made it to see me being baptized, and that memory means a lot to me.

I owe much of where I am today to the prayers of my elders, and I believe they would be very proud of the results of their prayers. To those who may not have embraced the faith yet, or to the new believers who are unsure of their path, know that there are people who have prayed for you, or are praying for you. I see myself as an answer to some of those prayers, here to equip individuals with varying levels of faith, whether they are still developing or just starting their spiritual journey.

I recall a moment when I questioned how I would use the skills and knowledge I've obtained in my life's journey. It's like a child wondering how school will benefit them in the future. The answer lies in countless ways.

I can help others navigate life with faith and confidence, with spiritual and natural knowledge.

Stewarding Someone Else's Property

In 2018, I embarked on a new chapter in my life with my husband. This significant change marked a fresh beginning, and it all started in a charming town called Chatsworth, Georgia. To give you a mental picture, Chatsworth is approximately twenty minutes away from Dalton, Georgia, and about thirty minutes from Ellijay, Georgia. It's nestled in the heart of Murray County. As we initiated our new journey in this area, numerous transitions and transformations unfolded.

In our new place, the landowner placed his trust in us. He recognized our dedication

Project Goshen and the Garden of Eden

and responsible stewardship of his property, which we were renting. He repeatedly assured us that the land was ours to care for and utilize as we saw fit because he had confidence in our commitment to maintaining it properly. We assured him that we would bring it back to life.

When we first arrived, he had already sold his forty chickens to us, as he was eighty years old and felt he could no longer manage them. I've always had the mindset of creating a homestead, and I believe this is where things began to connect for me regarding my project.

I had always aspired to create a homestead and engage in agricultural activities. I felt like I was born ready for this way of life. My upbringing contributed to this mindset, as my parents played a part in it. In fact, I recall a time when my father had chickens, rabbits, cows, and goats; so I was familiar with the basics.

I understood the importance of hard work and dedication. I remember a time when we didn't have a plow, and my sister Lynn and I got down on our hands and knees to till with whatever we had for tools and rid the arid soil of its weeds and their roots at a place in Buena Vista, Georgia. We planted potatoes with our father's assistance and later harvested the potatoes we had planted—again on our hands and knees, digging them up.

My upbringing was strongly influenced by my grandparents. Remember, Mamaw had a green thumb and could make flowers flourish, almost like what you'd see in a place

Project Goshen and the Garden of Eden

like Callaway Gardens. She had a special touch for bringing them back to life. From the moment I witnessed Mamaw praying over a bee sting, pleading the blood of Jesus over her finger and nurturing her flowers, invoking the Holy Ghost, singing songs of love for Jesus, and countless other actions, these memories were deeply put into my childhood mental archive. Now I'm determined to share these invaluable experiences with those who have been deprived of them.

Papaw was the expert when it came to the food part of gardening. Granny Jean would share her knowledge about the healing properties of various plants and the benefits of using natural remedies. I found this especially enjoyable because I could see the practical applications and demonstrations of these natural remedies. I never forget Granddaddy, a.k.a. W. R., always growing the tomatoes, catching the fish for fish fries, and going frog gigging. He was also a tree man; he knew all about them.

My mother made us kids cook and clean. It seemed like these chores were to prepare us for adulthood, ensuring we could become self-sufficient and not rely on others. While my father's military background exposed him to survival skills and the art of adaptability, it wasn't just about toughening up for combat. It's clear to me that the military experience instilled resilience and the ability to face life's challenges. Seeing that through my dad made me feel tough, like I had the know-how to survive and be self-sufficient. I remember a story Dad told us where he got in the mix of some disagreement between guys, whether it was in South Korea or Germany, I don't recall, and an officer had a billy stick and busted him across the head. And he needed to be sewn up for stitches with no pain medicine because he refused it. So then, for sure, I thought my dad was like Rambo and thought I had to be tough now.

They also taught us patience, to wait for something, and the joy of receiving it later was like a reward. We learned the value of not having something extra every day, which allowed us to truly appreciate it when we eventually received it. These experiences enriched our lives with gratitude and appreciation. Both of our parents emphasized the significance of self-reliance, so we wouldn't have to depend on anyone else. They guided us to be self-sufficient and not rely on conveniences, as did many aunts and uncles who influenced us as well, in many ways.

These many influences and lessons I absorbed as a child have collectively shaped my perspective and guided me on my life's journey, which has brought me to the bridge to fulfill this project Goshen.

Dedication to Helping Others

Writing this book not only aims to attract sponsorship for this project but also inspires me to develop e-courses on various topics, including gardening and spiritual teachings as well.

This project and mission is dedicated to helping others learn these principles and prosper in a manner aligned with faith. Life has evolved so much that many in my generation up to Gen Z lack basic skills like cooking and cleaning. I find myself creating motivational videos to inspire and instruct others on how to organize, clean, and manage everyday tasks. The downgrading of educational standards due to new guidelines in school systems, coupled with the neglect of encouraging diligence, is disheartening. The currency of laziness and the undermining of common sense underline the urgency for intervention! It's imperative to address the needs of the neglected in order to foster a more capable and informed society. Regrettably, a phrase I've often caught myself uttering since the late '90s is that "Common sense seems to be increasingly uncommon." It appears that the only thing commonly observed is the absence of common sense. I feel a calling to help and teach those who were neglected in learning these essential life skills. I believe that God has chosen me as one of the saints to impart this knowledge, promoting a life more abundant during our journey on this earth. We have the potential to prosper with the gifts He has given us all, within our reach, but our worldly mindset has been programmed to believe that we need government permission to attain these blessings.

I'm not saying to undermine authority; I'm suggesting that our minds have been influenced by worldly thinking that we can't reach for our blessings without some form of government's permission. This kind of mindset is misguided from desensitizing. I'm here to reemphasize that after the fall of humanity, we were meant to reclaim all the blessings because Jesus broke the curse on the tree. When He spoke the words "Speak life," He meant it. We have dominion over this world. I'm here to teach and help those who are still seeking the faith or have yet to reach certain levels of understanding. My purpose and drive is to guide them on how to survive in this world through God's principles, following a biblical and kingdom-focused way of living.

Once you gain wisdom and seek the Father and the Holy Spirit, you'll grasp the true meaning of dominion. I reiterate. You'll come to understand that the entire world can be your Goshen. We often lack wisdom for fearing man, and again, this is reemphasized.

Hosea 4:6 is where it's mentioned that God's people die due to a lack of knowledge. To truly gain understanding and decipher the true meaning behind the words and promises of the Lord. Again I express that we need to unravel the mysteries of the Bible to understand and then step into His original plan by exercising dominion over the world. Through the lens of scripture, we will discover the unwavering assurance that God's promises never return void. Christ's work on the cross redeemed us and broke the curse, allowing us to step into His original plan by exercising dominion over the world.

To those who haven't embraced the faith yet, there have been individuals praying for you, and prayers continue even now. If you're a new believer in Christ, steering over uncertainties and perhaps feeling overwhelmed, it may be because you haven't received proper indoctrination in the Word of God. Understanding the significance of not giving in to fear but trusting that the Lord will provide is crucial. *"For God hath not given us the spirit of fear; but of power, and of love, and of a sound mind" (2 Timothy 1:7).*

Whether these prayers originated from you or those who care about you, I sense a calling to be an answered prayer, offering guidance to individuals with varying levels of faith, whether they're new to this journey or wrestle with comprehension. There was even a time when I questioned how I could tackle these responsibilities, and now I am prepared to step into my purpose. With God's tremendous agape love, His Son suffered and died for us. I reiterate once again. I want Him to receive the full reward of His suffering. In doing so, we must rightly divide the word of God, apply, and teach others what it really meant for Him to come and redeem us. "For He made Him who knew no sin to be sent for us, that we might become the righteousness of God in Him" (2 Corinthians 5:21 NKJV). The verse highlights the concepts of atonement and righteousness through Jesus Christ. It emphasizes that Jesus, who was sinless, took on the sins of humanity so that those who believe in Him might be made righteous in the eyes of God.

Reaping and walking in what He paid for while on Earth means, "O fear the LORD, you his saints: for there is no want [lack] to them that fear him."

No lack. So according to God's Word, there's something wrong with saints of God doing without the necessities of life (i.e., needs). Jesus promised that God would feed and clothe all that were in covenant with Him. *Wants* fall under the category of "Is the thing I'm asking for in line with God's Word? And desire for me, and we must remember that God will never ever give us something to sin with or to replace Himself being God in our lives. This is the word in Hebrew and how it's defined in *Strong's Concordance* for *want* = H4270 *machso? makh-sore'*. From H2637, *deficiency*, hence impoverishment—lack, need, penury, poor, poverty, want (research and notes from PWD, a.k.a. Dad).

This is the beginning of wisdom

In 2 Corinthians 7:1, we find encouragement: "Because we have these promises, dear friends, let us cleanse ourselves from everything that can defile our body or spirit. And let us work toward complete holiness because we fear God." This sentiment resonates with the wisdom found in Proverbs 9:10, which states, "The fear of the Lord is the beginning of wisdom: and the knowledge of the Holy One is understanding." Additionally, Proverbs 4:6–7 reinforces this idea: "The beginning of wisdom is this: Get wisdom. Though it cost all you have, get understanding." These verses underscore the foundational importance of wisdom and understanding in our spiritual journey.

Being Wise

"After all, being wise isn't just about making the right decisions; it's about navigating life's challenges with discernment and vigilance."

Indeed, there's a vast difference between acting out of fear and acting wisely, as seen in the story of Joseph interpreting a dream in *Genesis 41:33–37*.

> "And now let Pharaoh look for a discerning and wise man and put him in charge of the land of Egypt. Let Pharaoh appoint commissioners over the land to

take a fifth of the harvest of Egypt during the seven years of abundance. They should collect all the food of these good years that are coming and store up the grain under the authority of Pharaoh, to be kept in the cities for food. This food should be held in reserve for the country, to be used during the seven years of famine that will come upon Egypt, so that the country may not be ruined by the famine."

The plan seemed good to Pharaoh and to all his officials. So Pharaoh asked

them "Can we find anyone
like this man, one in whom
is the spirit of God. (33–37)

After reflecting on Joseph's wise counsel to Pharaoh, it's evident that wisdom involves not only making advisable decisions for oneself but also extending guidance and caution to others, ultimately contributing to the greater good.

Being wise means listening to God's guidance, for as the Lord says, *"My sheep hear my voice, and I know them, and they follow me" (John 1:27).* You can either allow fear to drive you to hoard, or you can opt for wisdom, do what's right, and remain open to the potential for receiving greater blessings and opportunities.

If you're a true born-again saint, you'll be eager to learn what I have to teach because if you're a babe in Christ, you might not know these things. I believe the Lord sent me into the lives of those who are anxious, seeking knowledge, and willing to learn. I aim not only to teach them the practical aspects of growing things or natural remedies but also to guide them in their relationship with God. (See notes in garden section in back of book.) As we dive deeper into the principles of wisdom and faith, let us reflect on how these truths can guide us through challenging times and lead us to a life of abundance and fulfillment.

Noah's Stay on the Ark

- **Genesis 8:3–4** tells us that the waters receded for 150 days and the ark came to rest on the mountains of Ararat.
- **Genesis 8:5** says that the waters continued to decrease until the tenth month. On the first day of the month, the tops of the mountains were seen.

Total Duration:

- **Genesis 8:14** indicates that the earth was dry by the first day of the first month of Noah's 601st year—meaning, Noah was on the ark for a total of 377 days.

So Noah and his family on the ark, for example. They spent almost a year on the ark, relying on the provisions they brought with them and the faith they had in God's plan. Hold on to the concept of Noah on the Ark, and bear with me for a moment as I explain my idea for the Goshen project.

Part of Project Goshen includes Bible studies that will empower you to walk in prosperity and have faith that you can grow and cultivate from your own hands. God has given us dominion over the earth despite the fall of man in the garden, which was restored when the curse was broken at the cross. We have the opportunity to restore a garden of

Eden lifestyle on earth where God provides abundantly, and it's a matter of hunger and overcoming laziness, mentally and physically and with great faith.

It can be hard to explain at times, but when you grasp it, it's truly transformative. I can help you reach a point where you understand the depth of God's presence in us, His divine nature, and the incredible power that resides within us. I've learned things that have brought me to this point, and I'm excited to share them with you.

I genuinely believe I'm one of the called for such a time as this to lead the Goshen project. In a world where countless people are unaware and have adapted to the conveniences life offers with Christ slowly fading away, my mission is to rekindle their faith and knowledge. I am deeply grateful to the Lord Jesus Christ for enabling me to be one of the saints who have stopped to listen to His heartbeat, to discern when, how, and where to seek my education, and to engrave His teachings in the depths of my mind. While some who are lost or saints who have yet to attain full sanctification may find themselves in a state of fear and panic over impending events such as pandemics, wars, rumors of wars, empty stores, or vaccines, God is instilling established wisdom in those who seek it. These saints have diligently studied to show themselves approved. They are now being sent in, much like the Old Testament times of Goshen, to place the blood over the door like the Passover Lamb for protection. Although Christ had already died on the cross and risen again, He continues to restore what was lost due to the fall of humanity and the doubts and unbelief that may arise.

I'm driven by the love of God, and my goal is to not only own this property with my beloved spouse but to also conduct teaching sessions in Project Goshen. I aim to impart knowledge on planting seeds, harvesting, and recycling, especially for situations when stores might shut down and people may experience panic. Remember, this happens not from fear-mongering, but due to lack of faith.

It's not that God can't provide miraculously, but this is for individuals at varying levels of faith, including those who have sought healing and haven't received an immediate miracle, or those who still need medical attention. The purpose of this project is multifaceted, and I believe that someone's prayers have paved the way for this new Goshen, operating under a new covenant.

Project Goshen holds great significance for me because it serves as a platform to share the truth, to teach survival skills, to rekindle the knowledge of growing things, and above all, to remember the paramount importance of Jesus Christ. The world is currently desensitizing people from Christ, implementing various strategies to pull them away from Him. These tactics involve instilling fear, fostering the notion of a one-world government, and manipulating individuals into thinking they have no choice.

Project Goshen and the Garden of Eden

Reflecting on Purpose and Contemplating Alignment

Have you ever considered the importance of self-sufficiency in today's world? Project Goshen, under this new covenant, is designed to offer guidance. I plan to show how to raise seeds, harvest them, plant edible plants and gardens, and recycle seeds for continuous food production. It's a sustainable system that will never run out—just like the information and knowledge I want to share.

I will teach you how to cultivate seeds, harvest them, and even regrow edible plants by recycling the seeds through harvest. In Project Goshen, I aim to provide comprehensive guidance on sustainable agricultural practices. This includes not only the basic techniques of raising seeds and harvesting crops but also innovative methods for maximizing yield and minimizing waste. For instance, I'll dive into the intricacies of seed saving, teaching you how to carefully select, store, and reuse seeds from your harvests. By mastering these techniques, you'll not only ensure a steady food supply but also contribute to the long-term sustainability of your garden. Additionally, I'll explore the principles of permaculture and agroecology, showing you how to create resilient ecosystems that thrive without reliance on harmful chemicals. Through hands-on demonstrations and interactive workshops or e-courses I've created, you'll gain the knowledge and skills needed to cultivate a thriving garden that nourishes both body and soul which brings me back to Noah on the

Project Goshen and the Garden of Eden

Ark. You'll be able to grow food continually without running out. (Again, see notes in the back of the book on gardening.) This concept is similar to the story of Noah and his family spending nearly a year on the ark. What would it mean to truly live in alignment with God's principles? As we prepare to explore the spiritual dimensions of Project Goshen through Bible studies, let's take a moment to ponder: What does it mean to live in alignment with God's principles in our daily lives? And how can these principles guide us in our journey toward self-sufficiency? What does self-sufficiency truly mean in the context of our modern world? And how does it align with the principles outlined in God's word? During this time, they had to store food and supplies to last them throughout their stay.

They also had to care for the animals, ensuring they were fed and healthy. Inside the ark, they likely had different sections for living quarters, storage, and areas for the animals. It would have been a challenging and cramped living situation, but Noah and his family trusted in God's plan and cared for the creatures aboard until it was safe to leave the ark and repopulate the earth. The story of Noah and the ark is found in the book of Genesis chapters 6–9 in the Bible. Moreover, I'll offer Bible studies within the Goshen program. As soon as property becomes available, in Jesus name.) There you'll learn how to prosper and have faith in your ability to cultivate resources from your own hands. God has instilled in all of us the potential for dominion, but humanity's fall disrupted this harmony. And I believe in the restoration of the Lord!

> And after you have suffered a little while, the God of all grace, who has called you to his eternal glory in Christ, will himself restore, confirm, strengthen, and establish you. (1 Peter 5:10, "Through God's Grace, He Will Restore")

Paul was encouraging the church in Corinth:

> After you've been through some tough times, God, who

is full of grace and mercy, and who has invited you to share in His eternal glory through Jesus Christ, will personally bring you back, make you strong, firm, and steady. So, when life gets difficult and you're facing challenges, this verse encourages you to trust that God will see you through it all. He will not only help you endure, but He will also make you stronger and more resilient in the process. It's a reminder that God's grace is there to support you through every trial, and He will ultimately bring restoration and stability to your life. (1 Peter 5:10)

Here are the references that associate.

> Therefore we do not lose heart. Even though our outward man is perishing, yet the inward man is being renewed day by day. For our light affliction, which is but for a moment, is working for us a far more exceeding and eternal weight of glory, while we do not look at the things which are seen, but at the things which are not seen. For the things which

are seen are temporary, but the things which are not seen are eternal. (2 Corinthians 4:16–18 NKJV)

My brethren, count it all joy when you fall into various trials, knowing that the testing of your faith produces patience. But let patience have its perfect work, that you may be perfect and complete, lacking nothing. (James 1:2–4 NKJV)

And we know that all things work together for

good to those who love God, to those who are the called according to His purpose. (Romans 8:28 NKJV)

We are glad whenever we are weak but you are strong; and our prayer is that you may be fully restored.
Finally, brothers and sisters, rejoice! Strive for full restoration, encourage one another, be of one mind, live in peace. And the God of love and peace will be with you. (2 Corinthians 13:9–11)

> But seek first his kingdom and his righteousness, and all these things will be given to you as well. (Matthew 6:33 NKJV)

After discussing the principles of sustainable agriculture, Project Goshen will dive into the spiritual aspect of self-sufficiency, exploring how living in alignment with God's principles can lead to a more fulfilling and abundant life. By incorporating biblical teachings on stewardship, faith, and reliance on God's provision, participants will not only learn practical skills but also develop a deeper understanding of their relationship with the Creator and the natural world.

The MSGV of Matthew 6:33 says it like this: Steep your life in God-reality, God-initiative, God-provisions. Don't worry about missing out. You'll find all your everyday human concerns will be met. In other words, this verse teaches you that if you prioritize seeking God's kingdom and living righteously according to His ways, He will provide for all your needs. It's about making God the most important focus in your life, trusting Him to take care of you.

With God's wisdom, I want to help restore your faith and skills with such ability to walk in it! With God's wisdom, I'm driven to renew with steadfast faith and empower others to do the same! Let's embrace restoration and walk confidently in it! Bring me back from gray exile and put a fresh wind in my sales (Psalm 51:12 MSG)! In other words, bring back the happiness of knowing you've saved me and give me the strength to stay committed to you.

God Preparing Me in a Warning

In 2019, I clearly heard from the Lord that it was a "Shadrach, Meshach, and Abednego" moment. At first, I didn't fully grasp it, but as 2020 unfolded with the pandemic, scarcity of items, and various regulations, it began to make more sense. The challenges and uncertainties of those times made me reflect on the significance of the message from God and also reflect on the way I was brought up spiritually and educationally. In 2020, I faced certain challenges that prompted me to reflect on aspects of my upbringing. This reflection brought to mind specific instances and lessons I learned, particularly in spiritual matters. When churches shut down, I learned to focus more on God's word and promises, deepening my prayer life. This reliance on prayer ensured that we never faced financial dryness even as things were shutting down around us. Moreover, I discovered the strength that comes from leaning on God during difficult times. Despite the pandemic, I remained healthy, but I also learned how to pray fervently and remember some natural remedies for my spouse when he fell ill.

My life experiences, through the many challenges I've faced over the years, have led me to a point where I can guide and help others. It was as if God's response was clear—my purpose is to equip others with the wisdom and knowledge I've gained. This inspired me to create courses, essentially building bridges

Project Goshen and the Garden of Eden

for them so that they don't have to endure the same struggles I did to find the answers. These courses offer insights I've learned from various mentors and coaches, but my driving force is the love of God. Here are some notes and some examples of improvising and learning firsthand. My upbringing experiences enabled me to create courses offering guidance. I wanted to share the knowledge I gained so others wouldn't have to struggle and could easily navigate their own journeys. For example, I learned about natural remedies as a child, which helped with colds, flus, and other ailments. Additionally, I reflected on the way I was taught to pray, allowing me to rely on both these teachings for positive outcomes.

I chose the path of wisdom over fear and began my homestead journey by finding cost-effective alternatives to high-priced items. For example, instead of spending $12–$16 on a bottle of Tide, I started making my own homemade laundry soap. For a while, as a hobby and for experience.

I learned how to raise chickens for eggs. This way, I could have eggs and possibly trade them for other resources in a barter-and-trade system, like in the days of pioneers. Conversely, my grandparents' influence offered me a different set of skills, particularly in the areas of cooking and gardening. I learned from my grandmother (Granny Jean) how to prepare and cook food with love, experiencing the joy of family gatherings, laughter, hugs, and kisses around the dinner table.

Life has evolved so much that many in my generation lack basic skills like cooking and cleaning. I do this not only to teach but because I feel a calling to help those who were neglected in learning these essential life skills. I reiterate this once again because it is profound and necessary. I believe that God has chosen me as one of the saints to impart this knowledge, promoting a life more abundant during our journey on this earth. Now remember, this is according to one's faith. This is not fear-mongering but promoting a generation not to be lazy, to inspire us to co-labor with the Father and to gain life skills and become active. Additionally, it's about learning to activate the promises of God in Scripture. Therefore, you will be able to experience an abundant life in both practical and spiritual dimensions.

We have the potential to prosper with the gifts He has given us, all within our reach, but our worldly mindset has been programmed to believe that we need government permission to attain these blessings.

Remember, I touched on this earlier.

> Simon Peter, a bondservant and apostle of Jesus Christ,
>
> To those who have obtained like precious faith with us by the righteousness of our God and Savior Jesus Christ:
>
> Grace and peace be multiplied to you in the knowledge of God and

of Jesus our Lord, as His divine power has given to us all things that pertain to life and godliness, through the knowledge of Him who called us by glory and virtue, by which have been given to us exceedingly great and precious promises, that through these you may be partakers of the divine nature, having escaped the corruption that is in the world through lust. (2 Peter 1:1–4 NKJV)

Peter, who is writing this letter, is addressing fellow believers who share the same faith as him. He wishes them grace and peace through their knowledge of Jesus. Peter emphasizes that God has given believers everything they need to live a godly life through knowing Jesus and experiencing His power. This enables believers to escape the corruption caused by simple desires and to share God's divine nature. Folks, that means we get to partner and partake with Him in His divine nature. *Theias phuseos* in Greek (*theias*) means "nature" or "essence." In simpler terms, believers are able to share in and experience the qualities and characters of God Himself. So refer to the beginning of the book where I mentioned that walking in the qualities and characters of God Himself, life should be divine, supernatural, and/or His attributes associated with God such as being holy, which we should be since He has imparted to us His divine nature at salvation.

This approach prepares us for the challenges of these uncertain times—for those with a lack of faith or whatever your level of faith—by sending those with help and experience. And each time I asked, although it doesn't always come in the way we expect, the Lord loaded me up with what I needed. He allowed me to remember my elders, and parents and grandparents in church praying an hour before service every time, for the present and future. Which leads me to believe today that their prayers are why I carry the spiritual and practical wisdom I walk in today. Their prayers have undoubtedly shaped my journey and contributed to who I am now. And then the Father led me and Mateo to a place that was required for such a time like this, known as the North Georgia Revival as a result of our seeking and asking. We dove deeper into our prayer closet with the Lord, asking Him to increase our hunger for Him, to inspire us to pray, and to enable us to let go of the things we needed to release. Surrender was essential, as you need to make space for the new, by giving up something each day, just like dying daily and surrendering daily.

I aim to clarify my mission and goals for Project Goshen

Through my own research and experiences, I intend to assist others by providing practical skills, hands-on training, and e-courses. Additionally, I seek to foster spiritual growth and development. I will offer teaching through live sessions and videos, ensuring accessibility for all. Furthermore, I will provide contact information for those seeking further connection and support. I'm thankful for the way I was raised. It wasn't without its share of challenges, but everyone faces difficulties in their own way like I remember.

I learned what it's like to earn second or fifth place without throwing a tantrum. I understood that I needed to work harder. It wasn't a world where they'd bend over backward and hand you a first-place ribbon just because. That's mixed messaging. Our minds should be programmed to charge forward, train harder, improve, and be rewarded for our efforts. Unfortunately, the world has become overly sensitive and made life so comfortable. I learned that success isn't handed out easily, akin to the realization that earning second or fifth place without complaint taught me valuable lessons. These experiences have shaped my commitment to assisting others through practical skills and hands-on training. Just as I faced challenges and overcame them, I aim to foster growth and development. This journey is a testament to the importance of striving forward despite setbacks and embracing opportunities for personal and spiritual growth.

My project and mission is dedicated to helping others learn these principles and prosper in a manner aligned with faith. Life has evolved so much that many in my generation lack basic skills. Life has undergone considerable evolution, resulting in a noticeable deficit of fundamental abilities among individuals of the millennials to Gen Z. I don't want to believe they would suffer in survival skills, let alone manage everyday tasks. So realizing this, I've taken to producing motivational content aimed at guiding and empowering others to effectively manage and navigate everyday tasks and overall survival. I do this not only to teach but because I feel a calling to help those who were neglected in learning these essential life skills. I believe that God has chosen me as one of the saints to impart this knowledge. We have the potential to prosper with the gifts He has given us, all within our reach, but our worldly mindset has been programmed to believe that we need government permission to attain these blessings. In my journey, I've experienced the profound presence of God's promises and divine nature within me. Through the prayers of fellow saints and our collective connection through the Holy Spirit, I've witnessed the unfailing support of the great provider. His faithfulness has surpassed all expectations. When circumstances seemed dire and resources scarce, He orchestrated miraculous interventions. Saints attuned to His voice were instrumental, offering shelter, sustenance, love, employment, and countless provisions during times of need. These manifestations of divine care serve as a testament to His unwavering grace and the power of faith in action. I want to stop right here to thank some of those fellow saints: Lisa Baumgarth for taking us in with massive support, an advisor, and prayer warrior and team support from Shannon Tormoen. "I sought the Lord, and he answered me; he delivered me from all my fears" (Psalm 34:4). This verse reflects the idea of seeking God's guidance and experiencing His deliverance, which aligns well with the themes of divine intervention and provision in my testimony.

I remember the prayers being said and the dinners eaten at the table on little old Bragg Street, which was only a block or two from my mom's mom, Granny, that was on Clermont Road, even though it might not look the same now. I could go there and revisit millions of memories and instill the concept of the importance of prayer always. I believe God gave this vision to me to assist His children in this particular time, and in His still small voice in 2023, I heard there will be several pockets in this nation of Goshens to assist His children in need.

I once heard a story from one of my coach's colleagues, Trent Shelton. He's a famous football player, entrepreneur, speaker, author, and president of a Christian-based nonprofit organization called RehabTime. He shared an anecdote about his wife's glasses. He tried them on, and his reaction was, "Whoa, they're so strong!" His wife responded, "Honey, those are for my eyes. That's for my vision." This revelation made him realize that *his vision and her vision are not the same.*

Everyone has a unique vision. While these visions differ, mine connects with the Holy Spirit in diverse ways. Some may relate similarly, while others might not be in sync with your vision. This has led me to an understanding about my vision.

Strengthening the Community of Faith

Saints, by answering the prayers led by the Holy Spirit, we must act as protectors within Goshen under the new covenant, based on biblical standards, for those whose faith may be limited. We must provide support, whether it be in the form of giving medical assistance, teaching how to grow food, or filling various other needs, such as kingdom principles. An example speaking out the word. Calling out his promises, commanding things be. Speaking those things as though they were. Some might question whether this is "playing God," but it's not. God instills this wisdom within us because we asked for it and diligently studied His Word. We've searched into the content of the Scriptures, from Genesis to Revelation, and dissected the knowledge that He granted us. This includes breaking down the teachings of the Torah and studying the perspectives of the books of Moses.

We use this knowledge under the new covenant lens because it is a foreshadowing of divine information.

In other words, saints exist at different levels of faith. Back when Paul emphasized the need for all of us to support one another, that's exactly where our role comes into play (Ephesians 4:1–2 ESV).

So we should look out for one another and show an extra measure of love and grace. Paul directs us *"walk in a manner worthy of the calling to which you have been called, with all humility and gentleness, with patience, bearing with one another in love."*

We serve one another, assist, and mentor until individuals reach higher levels of faith. Furthermore, we also have the responsibility to teach and guide those who are new, like babes in Christ, as they embark on their spiritual journey until God's return.

Rediscovering Goshen

In the time of Moses, Goshen was a land of prosperity and refuge for the Israelites. It was a fertile region in ancient Egypt blessed with abundant resources and rich pastures. The descendants of Jacob, who came to be known as the Israelites, found comfort and sustenance in Goshen. The Israelites settled in Goshen. As the provisions were overflowing throughout the promised land, it was fertile ground for agriculture. Of course, when time passed, a change in leadership brought about oppression and hardship for the Israelites, but despite facing the adversities, the land of Goshen became a symbol of resilience and hope for the Israelites. It was this backdrop that made Moses emerge into the leader he was called to be, leading his people to the promised land. Goshen is intertwined with the book of Exodus, a remaining testament to the endurance and faith of a people destined for freedom. It is my husband's and my call to be the new Moses for this project and to reclaim dominion in the safe haven God created for His people.

Project Goshen and the Garden of Eden

Our reference story of Goshen and Moses is in the book of Genesis and the early chapters of Exodus. The particular passages would be *Genesis 45:10–11*; *Exodus 8:22, 9:26, 10:23,* and *12:22*. These passages describe the settlement of the Israelites in Goshen, their prosperity, and later, the events leading up to the Exodus from Egypt.

And that is exactly what my husband and I are trying to recapture in this era. Now how can I convince you of these things and lead you with God's favor, guiding you through different levels of faith? You might ask. It is my husband's and my call to be the new Moses for this project.

Let me share how I have witnessed this in action. I have prayed and spoken God's word back to Him, knowing it does not return void.

I said, "Lord, you know my heart's desires. I need property to start somewhere. I command that deeds, documents, and properties be given to me. Shortly after, a couple—one of which had been in dialogue with the Father—came to us and said, "The Lord told me to give you property, and I don't know why." I told him I don't know them, and He replied, "That's the neat thing. I know them." So in my heart, I knew the Lord heard me because He weighed my heart in how I asked Him. I told Him I need tools and testimonies to show His word in action.

This is just one of many examples I can't wait to share and teach. Listen to me: application is necessary. That was the intent of our Christ Lord and Savior anyways. The reason for writing this book is to witness the realiza-

Project Goshen and the Garden of Eden

tion of the potential in every state that God created, for us to walk in, because of what He died and rose for, and to appreciate the purpose behind all things created by Him.

A Glimpse of Gardening Techniques

Though it is said some people may misinterpret the Goshen error historical event as a sign that God will provide us with a sort of spiritual safe zone only, I believe that He does want our faith and for us to partner in an effort with the knowledge He provides. So that is when the realities of life happen; you will be able to rely on life's lessons to get us through by trusting in Him and the Holy Spirit, believing it will flourish. That kind of relationship with Him will make it possible. So let me summarize it like this. The importance of seeking wisdom and guidance from God to navigate life's challenges is profound, as it provides a foundation of faith and discernment that can guide decisions and actions with clarity and purpose. Many will find strength and resilience through their relationship with God and the lessons they have learned from their experiences. Trusting in God and cultivating a strong relationship with Him can indeed provide security and guidance as we face the ups and downs of life. With that said, a time of encouragement amid adversity will be needed and accepted.

Looking into the studies of James and the New Testament integrates true faith in everyday life experiences. His focus on having true faith must manifest itself in works of faith. He even goes on to stress faith endures trials and strong faith will face the challenge straight in the face and develop great endurance. Allow me to give credit where it's due for some of this survey to the study aid in *The New Open Bible, Study Edition* (1990) by Thomas Nelson Incorporation.

What am I saying? Faith allows the word to come alive and be active. Therefore, it is obedient to God's promises! See James 2:14–17. My friend's faith proves itself by works, so let's activate it and how we've been given the power to subdue it. Remember in 2 Peter 1:4, faith produces separation from the world and submission to God! When the Lord was downloading these things for me to write about, He told me there would be several pockets of these safe havens called Goshen across the nations. So other saints are listening as well as my friends. And we are all locking arms together as Paul says, "We

Project Goshen and the Garden of Eden

need one another." So remembering Goshen then, for now, in times of trouble, pray Psalm 91 over you and yours, under a new covenant lens, meaning they were hidden under His wings in the Old Testament. But under the new covenant, we are seated with Him in high places and not hidden. So begin to know your authority. Walk in it and pray in it that way. Amen! Thanks, Dad, for this teaching and revelation.

I'm very eager to start a live gardening course and e-gardening courses. I will leave you with some organic gardening tips here at the end of this book. I'm also putting out a gardening e-guide for educational purposes to thrive As it will collaborate with the e-gardening course called "Organic Gardening with a Spiritual Kiss" that I've created on mastermind.com, just look for Naomi Carmelo Hernandez as the author of that course on that platform. I want to leave you with a first basic lesson on Basic Gardening 101. My e-guide is listed on Amazon and Kindle under again author Naomi Carmelo Hernandez titled, *Organic Gardening for Beginners: A Comprehensive Guide to Year-Round Produce.*

Organic Gardening for Beginners

A Comprehensive Guide to Year-Round Produce

Garden Planting

Welcome to the world of organic gardening, where you can reap the benefits of fresh, homegrown vegetables. We'll explore the advantages of organic gardening, delve into why homegrown veggies are so essential, and give you a sneak peek into the planting timeline for your summer garden.

Importance of Homegrown Vegetables

Homegrown vegetables are unparalleled in flavor and nutritional value. By cultivating your own produce, you have control over the quality of your food. Plus, it's incredibly rewarding to enjoy the fruits (or rather, veggies) of your labor.

Notes

- When to plant veggies outside for an organic summer garden
- Preparing the garden
- Enhancing soil for optimal growth
- Choosing between raised beds and in-ground planting

Seed Starting

- Advantages of indoor seed starting
- Essential supplies for successful germination
- Matching veggies to your climate
- Complementary planting techniques

- *Superior flavor.* Homegrown vegetables taste fresher and more flavorful than store-bought ones.
- *Nutritional value.* Freshly harvested veggies retain more nutrients, offering better health benefits.
- *Control over pesticides.* You decide what goes into your garden, ensuring pesticide-free produce.

- *Reduced carbon footprint.* No need for transportation means a smaller environmental impact.
- *Gardening as a hobby.* Gardening is a relaxing and satisfying hobby that provides mental and physical benefits.

Overview of the Planting Timeline

Before we get our hands in the soil, it's crucial to understand when to plant your veggies. The planting timeline varies depending on your climate and the types of vegetables you want to grow.

Monthly Tasks and Activities

January

- Order seeds and supplies.
- Plan your garden layout.
- Start seedlings indoors (if required).

February

- Continue indoor seed starting.
- Test and amend garden soil.

March

- Transplant indoor seedlings.
- Direct sow cold-hardy veggies (e.g., peas, spinach).

April

- Continue transplanting seedlings.

- Start hardening off seedlings.
- Prepare garden beds and soil.

May

- Transplant warm-weather crops (e.g., tomatoes, peppers).
- Continue direct sowing (e.g., beans, cucumbers).
- Implement trellises or supports.

June

- Maintain garden (water, weed, mulch).
- Monitor for pests and diseases.

July

- Harvest early-ripening vegetables.
- Fertilize if necessary.

August

- Continue harvesting.
- Plan for fall planting.

September

- Harvest late-summer crops.
- Consider fall plantings (e.g., greens, radishes).

October

- Clean up the garden.
- Protect against early frosts.

November

- Prepare the garden for winter.
- Reflect on the season and make notes for next year.

Naomi Carmelo Hernandez

Notes for Next Year
Impact of Climate on Planting Dates

Climate greatly affects when you should start planting. Learn how to leverage your climate data to plan your garden's timeline effectively.

> *Early Spring (March–April).* Start planting cold-hardy vegetables as soon as the soil can be worked.
>
> *Late Spring (May–June).* Begin planting warm-weather crops after the last frost date.
>
> *Summer (June–August).* Maintain your garden during the growing season.

Early Fall (September). Consider fall planting of cool-season vegetables.

Late Fall (October–November). Prepare for the first fall frost and the end of the growing season.

So in Conclusion

In addition to the acre and a half that was given by God, we are still holding Him to His word for the tools that we need while showing great gratitude for what He's doing and has already done while commanding His Word for more property and a place for us to reside in and run as a safe haven. So be it in Jesus's name. My husband has already picked out the name for the small community because the property we're looking at has a residential home and another home on it. The name is Community House of Prayer, and the main home would be called the Harmony House. It has water resources and resources for homesteading. Also, with the other home, we could hold Bible classes based on biblical principles, offering a multitude of potential opportunities. I've been researching since 2015, and the project gained significant momentum in 2018. I started writing this book in September of 2023.

About the Author

Naomi S. Carmelo Hernandez is a mother, wife, entrepreneur, author, and mission volunteer who builds e-courses based on her life experience. Born in the great Peach State, where her background is rooted, Naomi at the age of 13 started the rest of her strong upbringing in the south area near a military base called Fort Benning, an hour south of Columbus, Georgia, that instilled resilience for her journey through this life, which reflects in her narrative. Growing up as a preacher's daughter, a preacher's granddaughter, and an army brat, her narratives are shaped not only by where and how she grew up but also by the spiritual teachings and the adaptive mindset instilled in her by her family and military upbringing.

Here is some contact information: naomicarmelo@gmail.com, web nch-carmelosroar.com, and https://www.facebook.com/naycarmelo or https://www.facebook.com/naomihercar.